hack
that
TOTE!

Mix & Match Elements to Create Your Perfect Bag

Mary Abreu

stashBOOKS.
an imprint of C&T Publishing

Text and artwork copyright © 2016 by Mary Abreu

Photography and artwork copyright © 2016 by C&T Publishing, Inc.

Publisher: Amy Marson

Creative Director: Gailen Runge

Editor: Liz Aneloski

Technical Editors:
Alison M. Schmidt and Del Walker

Cover/Book Design and
Style Photography: Page + Pixel

Production Coordinator:
Tim Manibusan

Production Editor:
Alice Mace Nakanishi

Illustrator: Mary Abreu and
C&T Publishing

Photo Assistant: Carly Jean Marin

Instructional Photography:
Diane Pedersen of C&T Publishing,
unless otherwise noted

Published by Stash Books, an imprint of C&T Publishing, Inc., P.O. Box 1456, Lafayette, CA 94549

Library of Congress Cataloging-in-Publication Data
Names: Abreu, Mary, author.
Title: Hack that tote! : mix & match elements to create your perfect bag / Mary Abreu.
Description: Lafayette, CA : C&T Publishing, Inc., [2016]
Identifiers: LCCN 2016003475 | ISBN 9781617452901 (soft cover)
Subjects: LCSH: Tote bags. | Sewing.
Classification: LCC TT667 .A34 2016 | DDC 646.4/8--dc23
LC record available at http://lccn.loc.gov/2016003475

Printed in China
10 9 8 7 6 5 4 3 2 1

There are many options for handles to use with each bag.

Pockets

Patch Pocket

Patch pockets are some of the simplest and most common types of pockets used in bag patterns, but they definitely have limitations. Because they are flat and are sewn to the bag on three sides, they don't hold much. Larger patch pockets can be divided with additional lines of stitching. All the patch pockets used in projects in this book are constructed similarly:

1. Match the interfaced and noninterfaced pocket pieces, right sides together, and sew the top and both sides. Do not sew the bottom of the pocket.

2. Clip the seam allowances at the sewn corners close to the stitch lines to reduce bulk. Turn right side out and press well.

3. Finish the bottom edge of the pocket with a serger, mock overlock stitch, or zigzag stitch close to the raw edge.

Sew top and both sides of pocket pieces, right sides together.

Finish bottom edge of pocket.

4. Place 1 exterior or lining piece right side up on a flat surface. Refer to the project instructions and measure up from the bottom edge and over from the left edge to determine the pocket placement. Align the bottom edge of the pocket with these marks. The top edge of the pocket will extend past the bottom edge of the exterior or lining piece.

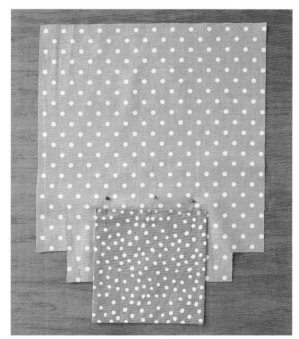

Place pocket on exterior or lining piece, aligning with measurements.

5. Pin the pocket in place. Sew ¼″ from the bottom edge of the pocket. Press the pocket up, covering the finished edge.

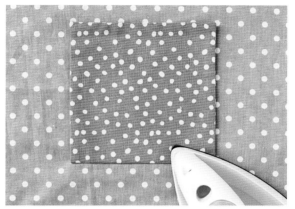

Press pocket over seam sewn in Step 5.

6. Sew along the sides of the pocket, close to the edge, from the top of the pocket to the bottom to secure it to the lining. Be sure to backstitch at the beginning and end of your stitches.

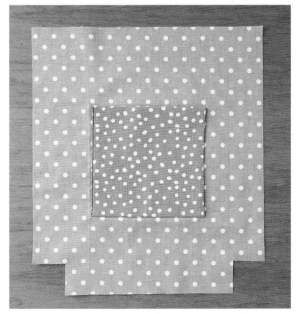

Sew close to edges of pocket from top edge to bottom.

Zipper Pocket

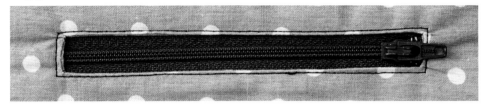

This pocket is one of my favorite touches on any bag pattern. It can be used inside or outside the bag, although it's best to use a piece of fabric that matches the outer pocket fabric in case any shows in the "window" of the zipper. All the projects in this book with zipper pockets are constructed in a similar manner:

1. On the wrong side of 1 zipper pocket piece, mark a ½″ rectangle (check the project instructions for dimensions and placement).

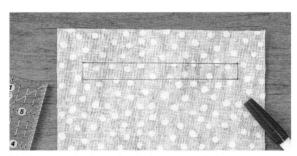

Mark rectangle through which zipper will show.

2. Place the marked zipper pocket piece on top of 1 interfaced exterior or lining piece, right sides together (check the project instructions for placement). Pin and sew on the rectangle you drew in Step 1.

Sew on rectangle drawn in Step 1.

3. Use a sharp pair of scissors to cut an opening in the middle of the sewn rectangle, stopping ¼″ from each side. Angle into each corner to cut, forming a Y shape. Take care not to cut into the stitches.

Cut through all layers, forming Y shapes in each corner.

4. Push the zipper pocket through the cut opening and press well, trimming away any thick interfacing as needed. Pin the edges of the zipper pocket to the exterior/lining.

Push fabric through opening and press.

5. Remove the zipper from the package and press with a medium iron.

6. Apply glue stick to the right side of the zipper tape and quickly center the zipper in the "window" you made in the exterior/lining. Press.

7. From the right side of the exterior/lining, use a zipper foot to sew all the way around the fabric "window" to secure the zipper in place. Be sure to move the zipper head out of the way.

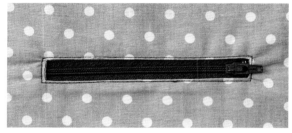

Stitch around zipper window to secure.

8. Flip over the exterior/lining and remove the pins holding the zipper pocket in place.

9. Match the right side of the remaining zipper pocket to the one that is already attached to the bag. You may need to trim to match the edges. Pin and sew around all 4 sides.

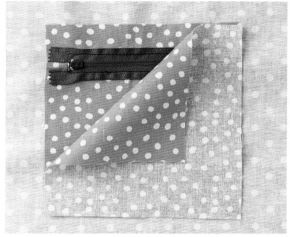

Match and pin zipper pockets before sewing.

Gusset Pocket

A pocket is cut larger than its finished dimensions and either gathered or pleated before being sewn to the bag. This creates a roomier option than its cousin, the patch pocket. For really large gusset pockets, you'll need to include some method for securing the top, such as hook-and-loop tape or an elastic casing (Boat/Pool Tote, page 68).

Decorative Elements

Fussy Cutting

Embroidery

Show off a favorite fabric by fussy cutting— placing the design within a specific area before cutting the fabric. The technique works well when using a single fabric or to frame a piece, for example, with a border print. I often will fussy cut fabrics to be used on pockets to really show off a design or to make a print line up across a seam.

A little bit of embroidery can make a big impact. Being a Southern girl, I'm a huge fan of monograms and love personalizing bags I make for others by adding their initials. Embroidery designs cover a range of styles and themes, making it easy to find just the right touch for any project. I invested in an embroidery machine a few years ago and love the speed with which it allows me to create thread art, but hand embroidery also remains a favorite, and it's a great alternative if you don't have the technology at your disposal.

Ribbon

Add a little ribbon for a quick pop of color or contrast by sewing a stripe horizontally or vertically on the body of the bag. Weave ribbons to make "fabric" panels and fuse them to interfacing before trimming to size. Lay ribbon in the middle of cotton canvas webbing and stitch along the long edges to secure for handles that wow. A touch of double-sided fusible web can help hold the ribbon in place before sewing.

Quilt Blocks

Leftover quilt blocks find new life when incorporated into bags or other projects. Add sashing or borders to make the blocks large enough for the cutting dimensions or alter the bag size to work with a quilt block you have on hand.

Leftover quilt blocks find new life as bags.

Extras

Key Catcher

There's nothing more irritating than having to dump out your bag to find your keys. A key catcher is an easy solution. Insert a piece of ribbon, some cotton twill tape, or a narrow piece of fabric (fold and sew similarly to the handles) through a latched swivel hook. Match the raw edges of the ribbon or fabric and sew through all the layers close to the hardware. Baste the raw edges together. Match the raw edges to the right side of a lining piece at the side seam, 2″–4″ down from the top edge. Proceed with the bag construction as directed.

Removable Bottom Insert

Designer fabric purses sold in boutiques and high-end department stores often include a removable bottom insert made with chipboard and covered in coordinating fabric. Make one for your bag by measuring the bag bottom after it's sewn. Add ¼″ to the length and width and cut two pieces of fabric to those measurements. Interface with woven fusible interfacing, if desired. Match the right sides together, pin, and sew both long sides and one short side with a scant ¼″ seam allowance. Press the unsewn edge ¼″ to the wrong side before turning the piece right side out. Measure the finished sleeve and cut chipboard, heavyweight craft stabilizer, plastic canvas, or any other suitable material slightly smaller than your measurements (I trim about ⅛″ smaller). Slide into the sleeve and sew closed. Insert the finished piece into the bottom of the bag after it's completely sewn.

Hard Bottom with Purse Feet

This feature requires a drill and a trip to the hardware store, but it's worth it! A hard bag bottom works best with a bag that includes a drop-in lining (Zip-Top Purse, page 88), or else be sure to leave a large enough gap in the lining through which to fit the board. You'll need to measure the bottom of the finished bag exterior and then have a piece of ⅛″-thick medium-density fiberboard (MDF) cut slightly smaller than those dimensions (I usually trim ⅛″ from the length and width measurements if I can't round down to a nice even number). Mark and drill holes to accommodate purse feet in all four corners (add a foot to the center if it's a particularly large bag; otherwise the center of the bottom may sag). Push the tip of an awl through the bag and the drilled holes for the purse feet. Apply a liquid seam sealant to the holes in the fabric and allow to dry before inserting the purse feet.

Heavyweight craft stabilizer inserted into fabric sleeve makes handy removable bottom insert for bags.

Purse feet attached to firm bottom keep bag off ground.

Hardware

Rings

Metal rings come in a variety of shapes (O, D, rectangle, triangle), finishes, and sizes. I use O-rings because they cause less friction against the fabric. You can use tabbed rings to attach handles and straps, or use with latched swivel hooks to make removable straps.

Grommets

The Drawstring Backpack (page 54) uses grommets to guide the drawstring cord, but they can be used in other ways, too. Drapery grommets positioned near the top edge of a bag can be used to anchor handles. Or use evenly spaced large grommets for feeding a drawstring to cinch closed a bag or even for wide ribbon to add a decorative touch.

Closures

A turn-lock clasp secures the flap of the Messenger Bag (page 74), but you could just as easily use a magnetic purse closure. Add flat magnets in sealed plastic to the inside of the Basic Tote Bag (I like this style of magnet because it puts less stress on the fabric and is less likely to rip out over time).

Buckles

Some projects use an adjustable slide buckle with a long strap, which is a great way to add carrying options to a bag. Consider using a metal buckle with a post and grommets to make an adjustable belt-style strap or handles. Nylon or plastic parachute buckles also make great closures or detachable/adjustable strap options.

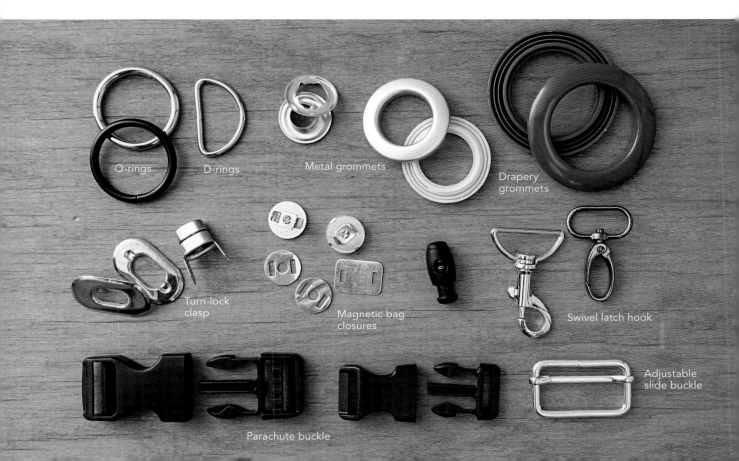

O-rings
D-rings
Metal grommets
Drapery grommets
Turn-lock clasp
Magnetic bag closures
Swivel latch hook
Parachute buckle
Adjustable slide buckle

basic tote bag

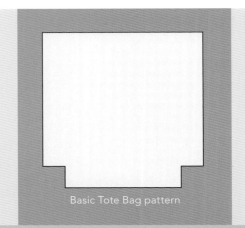

Basic Tote Bag pattern

FINISHED BAG: 12½″ wide × 15″ high × 5″ deep

Materials

Yardage is based on 42″ width of fabric unless stated otherwise.

FABRIC

- ⅝ yard for exterior
- ⅝ yard for lining
- ¼ yard for handles
- 1 fat quarter for pocket

INTERFACING

- 2¼ yards woven fusible interfacing, 20″ wide
- 1⅛ yards medium-weight fusible interfacing, 20″ wide

Cutting

EXTERIOR

- Cut 2 squares 18″ × 18″. Cut 1 square 2½″ × 2½″ from each bottom corner.

LINING

- Cut 2 squares 18″ × 18″. Cut 1 square 2½″ × 2½″ from each bottom corner.

PATCH POCKET

- Cut 2 squares 9″ × 9″.

HANDLES

- Cut 1 rectangle 6″ × 42″.

WOVEN FUSIBLE INTERFACING

- Cut 2 squares 18″ × 18″. Cut 1 square 2½″ × 2½″ from each bottom corner.
- Cut 1 square 9″ × 9″.
- Cut 1 rectangle 3″ × 42″.

HEAVYWEIGHT FUSIBLE INTERFACING

- Cut 2 squares 18″ × 18″. Cut 1 square 2½″ × 2½″ from each bottom corner.

Pattern Tip

If you prefer to use a paper pattern rather than cutting the fabric pieces by their dimensions as shown in the cutting list, you can use pattern-tracing material (Pattern Ease, Easy Pattern, Swedish Tracing Paper, and so on). Use a ruler and pen to mark an 18″ × 18″ square. Then, mark a 2½″ × 2½″ square at each of the bottom corners. Cut out the pattern and use it to cut out the bag body pieces.

Construction

All seam allowances are ¼˝ unless otherwise noted. Refer to Anatomy of the Tote Bag Pattern (page 8) and the Glossary (page 99) as needed.

1. Follow the manufacturer's directions to fuse the corresponding woven fusible interfacing pieces to the wrong side of each exterior piece and 1 pocket piece. Fuse medium-weight fusible interfacing to the wrong side of each lining piece.

2. Match the exterior bag pieces, right sides together. Pin the sides and bottoms. Sew. Do not sew the corner cutouts yet. Press open the seams. **FIG. A**

3. Create the bottom corners of the tote bag by matching a side seam to the bottom bag seam.

Pin and sew in a straight line. Repeat with the opposite corner. Turn right side out and set the bag aside. **FIG. B**

4. See Patch Pockets (page 28) to make 1 patch pocket. Sew the pocket to a lining piece, positioning it 4½˝ up from the bottom edge and 4¾˝ from the left edge.

5. Repeat Steps 2 and 3 to assemble the lining, but leave a 5˝ gap in the bottom of the lining for turning the bag right side out. Set it aside.

A. Match exterior bag pieces, right sides together.

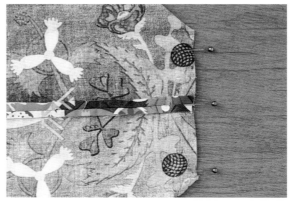

B. Match side seam and bottom seam, right sides together, to form bag corners.

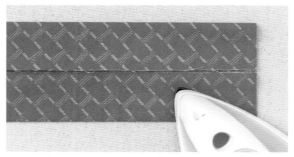

C. Press long, raw edge of handles toward middle, wrong sides together.

D. Place interfacing in middle of strap before refolding and fusing.

6. Press the handles rectangle in half, wrong sides together, matching the long edges. Open up the rectangle and press both long edges toward the middle crease, wrong sides together. The raw edges should be inside the handles. **FIG.C**

7. Open the handle and place the woven fusible interfacing in the middle of the strap with the fusible side against the wrong side. Refold and press to fuse. **FIG.D**

8. Fold the handle in half again lengthwise so the raw edges are inside. Stitch close to the edge along the long open edge of the handle. Repeat on the folded edge. Optional: Add a second line of topstitching inside each previous line.

9. Find the middle of the handle and cut it in half, so you have 2 equal-length pieces.

10. Pin a handle in place on each side of the bag, 4˝ in from each side seam, matching both raw ends with the top of the bag. The handles should make U-shapes against the body of the tote bag. Baste in place. **FIG.E**

11. Slip the exterior into the lining, right sides together, and match the top edges of the bags. Make sure the handles are tucked between the bag exterior and lining. Pin, matching the side seams, and sew. **FIG.F**

12. Turn the bag right side out through the gap in the lining. Press well, making sure the lining is fully tucked inside the bag.

13. Topstitch around the top of the bag, ⅛˝ from the edge. **FIG.G**

14. Slipstitch or machine stitch the gap in the lining closed.

E. Pin handles to bag exterior, 4˝ from each side seam.

F. Insert bag exterior and handles into bag lining, right sides together.

G. Topstitch around top edge of bag.

goodie bag
with Reverse Appliqué

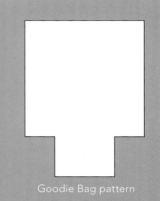

Goodie Bag pattern

FINISHED BAG: 5¼″ wide × 10″ high × 7″ deep

Materials

Yardage is based on 42″ width of fabric unless stated otherwise.

QUILTING COTTON:
- ½ yard for exterior and handles
- ⅜ yard for lining

FABRIC SCRAP: 5¼″ × 5¼″ for reverse appliqué background

INTERFACING:
- ¾ yard woven fusible interfacing, 20″ wide
- ¾ yard heavyweight fusible interfacing, 20″ wide

FUSIBLE WEB: 5″ × 5″ scrap of paper-backed fusible web

Cutting

See Pattern Tip (page 36).

EXTERIOR
- Cut 2 rectangles 12¾″ × 14″. Cut 1 square 3½″ × 3½″ from each bottom corner on a 12¾″-long side.
- Cut 1 square 6″ × 6″.
- Set aside a scrap at least 5″ × 5″ for the appliqué initial.
- Cut 2 rectangles 4″ × 12¾″ for the handles.

LINING
- Cut 2 rectangles 12¾″ × 14″. Cut 1 square 3½″ × 3½″ from each bottom corner.

WOVEN FUSIBLE INTERFACING
- Cut 2 rectangles 12¾″ × 14″. Cut 1 square 3½″ × 3½″ from each bottom corner on a 12¾″-long side.
- Cut 2 rectangles 2″ × 10″ for the handles.

HEAVYWEIGHT FUSIBLE INTERFACING
- Cut 2 rectangles 12¾″ × 14″. Cut 1 square 3½″ × 3½″ from each bottom corner on a 12¾″-long side.

Inside the / **hack**

The Goodie Bag is a scaled-down version of the Basic Tote Bag (page 36) and finishes with an almost squared-off shape to accommodate a variety of party favors. The reverse appliqué window allows for personalization.

All seam allowances are ¼˝ unless otherwise noted. Refer to Anatomy of the Tote Bag Pattern (page 8) and the Glossary (page 99) as needed.

1. Using your computer, print a mirror image of an initial no longer than 4˝ on any side.

2. Trace the initial onto the fusible web. Fuse it to the wrong side of an exterior fabric scrap and cut it out. **FIG.A**

3. Fuse the initial appliqué to the right side of the 5¼˝ × 5¼˝ background square, centering the design. Stitch around the edge of the appliqué as desired. Set it aside. **FIG.B**

4. Use a compass to draw a 4¾˝ circle or trace a CD or DVD in the center of the wrong side of the 6˝ × 6˝ exterior square. **FIG.C**

5. Place the 6˝ × 6˝ square on 1 exterior piece, right sides together, centered and 1½˝ down from the top edge. Pin. Sew directly on the circle drawn in Step 4, through both layers of fabric.

6. Trim inside the circle, approximately ⅛˝ from the stitching, to create a "window." **FIG.D**

A. Trace initial onto fusible web.

B. Stitch around appliqué.

C. Trace circle for appliqué window.

D. Trim center of appliqué window.

7. Push the fabric through the circle and press to the wrong side, forming a clean edge for the appliqué window. **FIG. E**

8. Center the appliquéd background square in the window, with the right side of the appliqué against the wrong side of the exterior. Pin. Sew close to the finished edge of the circle. **FIG. F**

9. Follow the manufacturer's directions to fuse the corresponding woven fusible interfacing to the wrong side of each bag exterior piece. Fuse the heavyweight fusible interfacing to each bag lining piece.

10. Match the exterior bag pieces, right sides together. Pin the sides and bottoms. Sew. Press open the seams. **FIG. G**

11. Create the bottom corners of the bag by matching a side seam to the bottom bag seam. Pin and sew in a straight line. Repeat with the opposite corner. Turn right side out and set the bag aside. **FIG. H**

12. Repeat Steps 10 and 11 to assemble the lining, but leave a 3˝ gap in the bottom of the lining to turn the bag right side out. Set the lining aside.

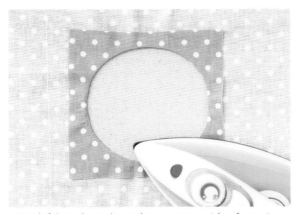

E. Push fabric through window to wrong side of exterior.

F. Sew around appliqué window through all layers.

G. Match exterior bag pieces, right sides together.

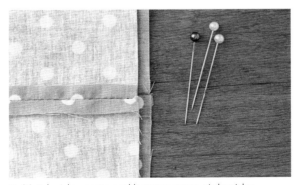

H. Match side seams and bottom seam, right sides together, to form bag corners.

13. Press 1 handle rectangle in half, wrong sides together, matching the long edges. Open up the rectangle and press both long edges toward the middle crease, wrong sides together. The raw edges should be inside the handle.

14. Open the handle and place a woven fusible interfacing rectangle in the center. Refold the handle over the interfacing and press to fuse. Fold and press in half lengthwise so raw edges are hidden in the center again. **FIGS. I–K**

15. Stitch close to the edge along the long open edge of the strap. Repeat on the folded edge.

16. Repeat Steps 13–15 with the second handle.

17. On both exterior sides, pin the handles in place 4″ in from the side seams, matching the raw ends with the top of the bag. The handles should make U-shapes against the body of the bag. Baste in place. **FIG. L**

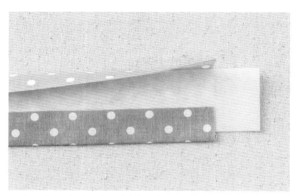

I. Place interfacing in middle of strap before refolding.

J. Fold handle over interfacing and fuse.

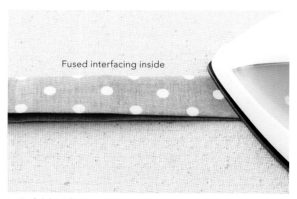

Fused interfacing inside

K. Refold and press again on previous folds.

18. Slip the bag exterior into the bag lining, right sides together, and match the top edges of the bags. Make sure the handles are tucked between the bag exterior and lining. Pin, matching the side seams, and sew. **FIG. M**

19. Turn the bag right side out through the gap in the lining. Press well, making sure the lining is fully tucked inside the bag.

20. Topstitch around the top of the bag, 1/8˝ from the edge. **FIG. N**

21. Slipstitch or machine stitch the gap in the lining closed.

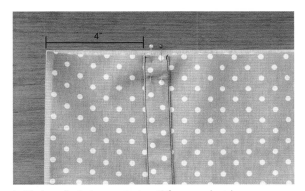

L. Pin handle to bag exterior, 4˝ from each side seam.

M. Insert bag exterior and handles into bag lining, right sides together.

N. Topstitch around top edge of bag.

wine-bottle *bag*

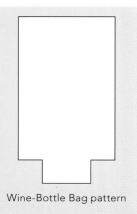

Wine-Bottle Bag pattern

FINISHED BAG: 4″ wide × 13¼″ high × 4½″ deep

Materials

Yardage is based on 42″ width of fabric unless stated otherwise.

FABRIC: 2 fat quarters

WOVEN FUSIBLE INTERFACING: ½ yard, 20″ wide

RIBBON: ½ yard, 1″ wide

Cutting

See Pattern Tip (page 36).

EXTERIOR
- ☐ Cut 2 rectangles 9″ × 16″. Cut 1 square 2¼″ × 2¼″ from each bottom corner.

LINING
- ☐ Cut 2 rectangles 9″ × 16″. Cut 1 square 2¼″ × 2¼″ from each bottom corner.

INTERFACING
- ☐ Cut 4 rectangles 9″ × 16″. Cut 1 square 2¼″ × 2¼″ from each bottom corner.

Inside the / **hack**

Remove the handles and adjust the proportions to convert the Basic Tote Bag (page 36) into this Wine-Bottle Bag. Buttonholes and a double row of stitches through both layers of the bag create a casing for ribbon to add that gift-giving touch.

All seam allowances are ¼″ unless otherwise noted. Refer to Anatomy of the Tote Bag Pattern (page 8) and the Glossary (page 99) as needed.

1. Follow the manufacturer's instructions to fuse the woven fusible interfacing to the wrong sides of the exterior and lining pieces of the bag.

2. Follow the instructions in your sewing machine manual to sew 2 buttonholes ¾″ long on the right side of 1 exterior bag piece, 3″ in from each side and 3″ down from the top edge. Cut open the buttonholes and apply a small amount of seam sealant (optional) to inhibit fabric fraying. **FIG.A**

3. Match the exterior pieces, right sides together. Pin the sides and bottom edges. Sew. Press open the seams. **FIG.B**

4. Create the bottom corners of the bag by matching a side seam to the bottom seam, right sides together. Pin and sew in a straight line. Repeat with the opposite corner. **FIG.C**

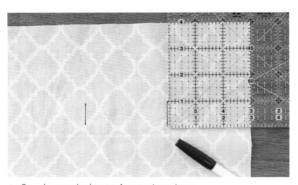

A. Sew buttonholes to 1 exterior piece.

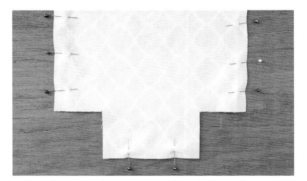

B. Match exterior bag pieces, right sides together.

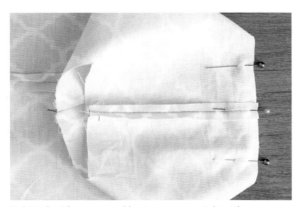

C. Match side seam and bottom seam, right sides together, to form bag corners.

D. Place exterior into lining, right sides together.

5. Repeat Steps 3 and 4 with the lining pieces, leaving a 3″ gap in the center of the bag bottom for turning.

6. Insert the exterior into the lining, right sides together. Match the top edges of the bag. Pin and sew. **FIG.D**

7. Turn the bag right side out through the gap left in the lining. Tuck the lining into the exterior and press.

8. Machine stitch or slipstitch the gap in the lining closed.

9. Topstitch ⅛″ from the top edge of the bag all the way around.

10. To make the casing, stitch all the way around the bag 2⅝″ from the top edge. Make a parallel line of stitches 3⅞″ from the top edge of the bag (1¼″ away from the previous line of stitches). **FIG.E**

11. Use a bodkin or attach a safety pin to the end of the ribbon and feed the ribbon through the buttonholes and the casing. Tie the ribbon ends into a bow.

E. Stitch parallel rows around top of bag.

nested boxes

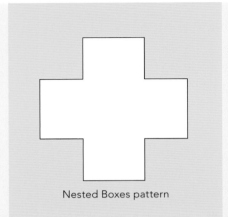

Nested Boxes pattern

SMALL BOX: 4½″ wide × 3¼″ high × 4½″ deep

MEDIUM BOX: 5¾″ wide × 4⅛″ high × 5¾″ deep

LARGE BOX: 7″ wide × 5″ high × 7″ deep

Materials

Yardage is based on 42″ width of fabric unless stated otherwise.

QUILTING COTTON:

☐ For 1 box (any size): 1 fat quarter for exterior and 1 fat quarter for lining

☐ Or, for 3 boxes (1 box in each size): ⅞ yard for exterior and ⅞ yard for lining

HEAVYWEIGHT CRAFT STABILIZER:

☐ For 1 box: *Small:* ⅓ yard; *Medium:* ½ yard; *Large:* ⅝ yard

☐ Or, for 3 boxes (1 box in each size): 1 yard total

NOTE: This pattern is best suited for nondirectional prints.

Cutting

See Pattern Tip (page 36).

EXTERIOR

☐ **Small:** Cut 1 square 11½″ × 11½″. Cut 1 square 3¼″ × 3¼″ from each corner.

☐ **Medium:** Cut 1 square 14½″ × 14½″. Cut 1 square 4⅛″ × 4⅛″ from each corner.

☐ **Large:** Cut 1 square 17½″ × 17½″. Cut 1 square 5″ × 5″ from each corner.

LINING

☐ **Small:** Cut 1 square 11½″ × 11½″. Cut 1 square 3¼″ × 3¼″ from each corner.

☐ **Medium:** Cut 1 square 14½″ × 14½″. Cut 1 square 4⅛″ × 4⅛″ from each corner.

☐ **Large:** Cut 1 square 17½″ × 17½″. Cut 1 square 5″ × 5″ from each corner.

INTERFACING

☐ **Small:** Cut 1 square 11″ × 11″. Cut 1 square 3¼″ × 3¼″ from each corner.

☐ **Medium:** Cut 1 square 14″ × 14″. Cut 1 square 4⅛″ × 4⅛″ from each corner.

☐ **Large:** Cut 1 square 17″ × 17″. Cut 1 square 5″ × 5″ from each corner.

Construction

All seam allowances are ¼" unless otherwise noted. Refer to Anatomy of the Tote Bag Pattern (page 8) and the Glossary (page 99) as needed.

1. Fold the exterior in half diagonally, right sides together, matching the corner cutouts. Pin and sew. Clip the corners at the bottom and press the seams open. **FIG. A**

2. Repeat Step 1 with the opposite exterior corners. Set aside. **FIG. B**

3. Repeat Steps 1 and 2 with the lining.

4. Fold and press the top edge of both the exterior and lining over ¼" to the wrong side. Turn the exterior box right side out. **FIG. C**

5. Use a ruler to fold up and crease all 4 of the extended arms of the interfacing piece.

6. Insert the stabilizer box into the exterior, folding the sides up along the creases made

A. Fold exterior in half diagonally and match corners.

B. Match opposite box corners.

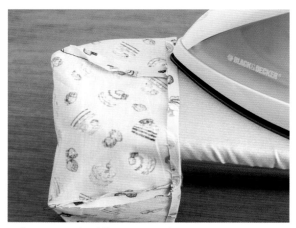

C. Press top edge ¼" to wrong side.

in the previous step. Tuck the upper edges of the stabilizer inside the folded top edge of the exterior.

7. Place the lining, wrong side out, inside the interfaced exterior box. Match and clip or pin the top edges of the box together. **FIG. D**

8. Topstitch close to the top edge, all the way around the box.

D. Match and clip top edge of box.

Inside the / **hack**

By starting with a square and adding a second set of corner notches, the Basic Tote Bag (page 36) takes on a decidedly boxy shape. Scale up or down to make the size suitable for your needs.

drawstring **backpack**

Drawstring Backpack pattern

FINISHED BACKPACK: 16″ wide × 21¼″ high

Materials

Yardage is based on 42″ width of fabric unless stated otherwise.

FABRIC: 1 yard for exterior

INTERFACING: ⅛ yard heavyweight double-sided stiff fusible interfacing or stabilizer (such as fast2fuse HEAVY Interfacing, by C&T Publishing)

CORDING: 4¼ yards, ⅛″–¼″ diameter

GROMMETS: 2 at 1″ diameter

Cutting

See Pattern Tip (page 36).

Tip

Adapt this pattern for lighter-weight fabrics by flat lining (page 100) the exterior with a heavier fabric, such as canvas.

EXTERIOR

☐ **Body:**
  Cut 2 rectangles 17″ × 22″.

☐ **Drawstring casings:**
  Cut 2 rectangles 1½″ × 17″.

☐ **Cord guides:**
  Cut 2 rectangles 3″ × 4″.

FUSIBLE INTERFACING

☐ **Cord guides:**
  Cut 2 rectangles 1½″ × 2½″.

Inside the / **hack**

Eliminating the cut-out corners of the Basic Tote Bag (page 36) creates a flatter bag. A drawstring casing at the top edge and tabs with grommets work together to make this bag function like a backpack.

Construction

All seam allowances are ¼″ unless otherwise noted. French seams (page 100) eliminate the need for a lining. Refer to Anatomy of the Tote Bag Pattern (page 8) and the Glossary (page 99) as needed.

1. Press the cord guides in half, right sides together, matching the short edges. **FIG. A**

2. Sew the short sides. Turn right side out and press.

3. Slip the fusible rectangles into the cord guides. Press to fuse. **FIG. B**

4. Place 1 cord guide on the bottom left corner of an exterior piece, ⅝″ up from the bottom, with the raw edges even on the left-hand side. Baste. Repeat on the opposite side with the remaining cord guide. **FIG. C**

5. Match the bag exterior pieces, *wrong* sides together. Pin the sides and bottom. Sew. Trim the seam allowance to ⅛″. **FIG. D**

6. Turn the bag right sides together and press the seam flat.

A. Match cord guides, right sides together.

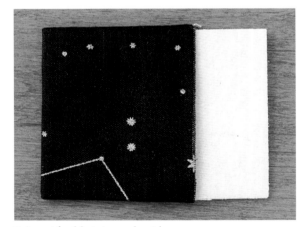

B. Insert fusible into cord guides.

Baste ⅝″ up.

C. Baste cord guides to exterior.

D. Match exterior bag pieces, *wrong* sides together.

7. Sew the seams a second time, capturing the trimmed seam allowances inside the stitching, to create a French seam (page 100). Press. Leave the bag wrong side out and set it aside. **FIG. E**

8. Match the short ends of the drawstring casing, right sides together, and pin. Using a ½˝ seam allowance, sew the first and last ½˝ along the short end, leaving a ½˝ gap in the stitching to create the opening for the

drawstring. Make sure to backstitch at the beginning and end of each line of stitches. **FIG. F**

9. Press open the seams. Press under the raw edge of the seam allowance. **FIG. G**

10. From the right side of the drawstring casing, topstitch along the seam allowances on both sides. Repeat on the other drawstring casing side seam. **FIG. H**

11. Press 1 raw edge of the drawstring casing ¼˝ to the wrong side.

E. Sew seams second time to create French seam.

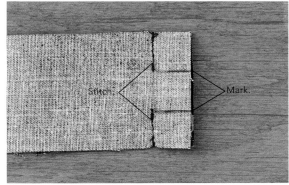

F. Match short ends of drawstring casing, leaving ½˝ gap.

G. Press under raw edge of seam allowance.

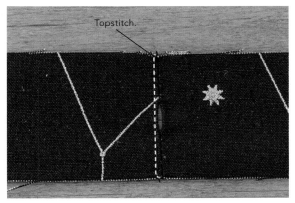

H. Topstitch along seam allowance.

12. Match the unpressed edge of the right side of the drawstring casing to the top edge of the wrong side of the backpack. Pin, starting at the side seams. Sew. Trim the seam allowance to ⅛″. **FIG. I**

13. Press the drawstring casing over the seam allowance and flat against the top of the backpack. Pin and sew close to the folded bottom edge of the drawstring casing. **FIG. J**

14. Topstitch around the top edge of the drawstring casing.

15. Follow the manufacturer's instructions to install the grommets in the center of each cord guide. **FIG. K**

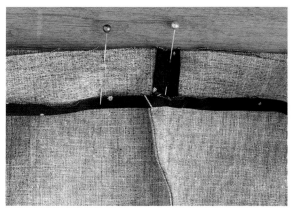

I. Match drawstring casing to top edge of backpack.

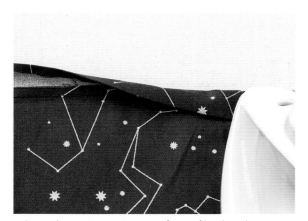

J. Press drawstring casing over front of backpack.

K. Install grommets in cord guide.

16. Cut the cord into 2 equal-length pieces. Set aside 1 piece. Use a bodkin or safety pin to feed 1 cord piece through the bottom of the cord guide, up through the bag front drawstring casing (from the left), around through the bag back drawstring casing (from the right), and then back down to the starting point. Knot. Repeat on the opposite side of the bag.

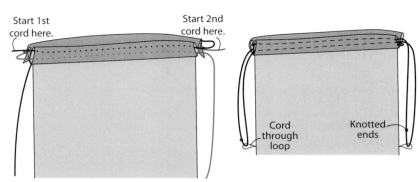

Run cord through cord guide and drawstring casing.

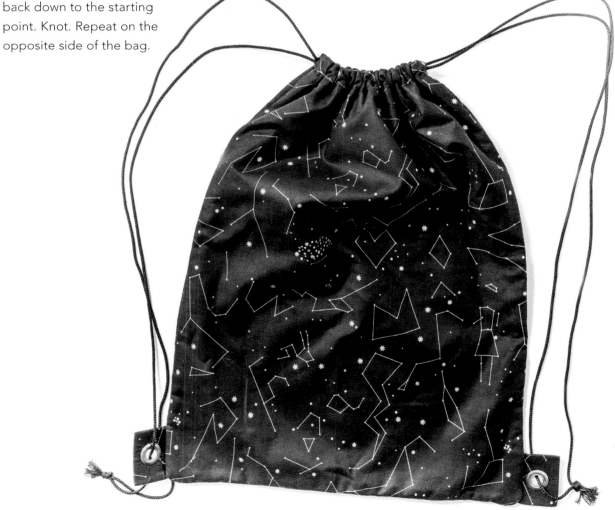

tubular frame purse

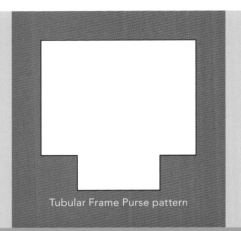

Tubular Frame Purse pattern

FINISHED PURSE: 9¾″ wide × 14¼″ high × 9″ deep

Materials

Yardage is based on 42″ width of fabric unless stated otherwise.

FABRIC:

☐ 1 yard for exterior

☐ ⅝ yard for lining

☐ ¼ yard for handles

☐ ⅓ yard for patch pockets

INTERFACING:

☐ ⅝ yard foam interfacing, 60″ wide (or 1⅛ yards, 20″ wide)

☐ 1⅓ yards fusible woven interfacing, 20″ wide

BUCKRAM: 1⅛ yards, 20″ wide

CORDING: 1½ yards 1¼″-diameter cotton cording

ZIPPER: 10″–14″ long

PURSE FRAME: 12″ tubular purse frame

OPTIONAL: 9″ × 10″ piece of leather, suede, faux leather, or vinyl for bag bottom, if desired

Tip

I loved quilting the exterior bag pieces for this purse. If you choose to do the same, I recommend cutting the foam interfacing and exterior pieces about 2″ larger than called for and then trimming them to size after quilting.

Inside the / **hack** ------------------

This purse looks dramatically different from the Basic Tote Bag (page 36), and yet the pattern is nearly identical. A casing for the tubular purse frame and dimensional handles that look store-bought are the keys to the transformation.

If you have a different-size tubular frame, you can adjust the dimensions to fit your frame. Simply measure the short leg of the frame to the bend to calculate the corners. Measure across the top of the frame for the bag width, adding the corners and seam allowances to determine the cut size.

All seam allowances are ¼″ unless otherwise noted. Refer to Anatomy of the Tote Bag Pattern (page 8) and the Glossary (page 99) as needed.

Cutting

See Pattern Tip (page 36).

EXTERIOR

☐ Cut 2 squares 19¼″ × 19¼″. Cut 1 square 4½″ × 4½″ from each bottom corner.

☐ **Zipper pocket:** Cut 2 squares 12″ × 12″.

☐ **Tubular frame casing:** Cut 2 rectangles 3″ × 18¼″.

LINING

☐ Cut 2 squares 19¼″ × 19¼″. Cut 1 square 4½″ × 4½″ from each bottom corner.

HANDLES

☐ Cut 2 rectangles 4″ × 28″.

PATCH POCKETS

☐ Cut 4 squares 10″ × 10″.

FOAM INTERFACING AND BUCKRAM

☐ Cut 2 squares 19¼″ × 19¼″. Cut 1 square 4½″ × 4½″ from each bottom corner.

FUSIBLE WOVEN INTERFACING

☐ **Patch pockets:** Cut 4 squares 10″ × 10″.

☐ **Handles:** Cut 2 rectangles 4″ × 28″.

☐ **Tubular frame casing:** Cut 2 rectangles 3″ × 18¼″.

1. Baste the foam interfacing to the wrong sides of the exterior bag pieces and baste the buckram to the wrong sides of the lining pieces. Follow the manufacturer's directions to fuse the woven fusible interfacing to the wrong sides of the corresponding pocket, handles, and tubular frame casing pieces.

2. Use the 12″ × 12″ zipper pocket squares to make a zippered pocket (page 30) on 1 exterior piece with a ½″ × 10″ rectangular window, 1½″ down from the top edge and 1″ in from each side.

3. Match the long edges of a handle, right sides together. Pin and sew. Center the seam and press open. **FIG. A**

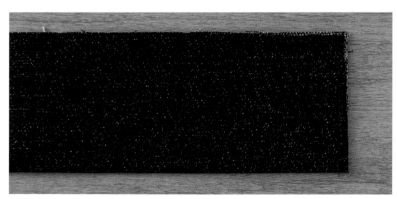

A. Match long edges of handle, right sides together.

4. Turn the handle right side out with a turning tool. Press. Finish the short edges with a zigzag stitch or serger.

5. Fold the handle in half with the seam centered inside, matching the long edges, and pin. Starting and stopping 3″ from each end, topstitch close to the long edge to secure. **FIG.B**

6. Cut the cording into 2 pieces 21½″ long. Wrap the cut ends with a small amount of masking tape. Apply a small amount of a liquid seam sealant to the cut edges.

7. Use a bodkin or safety pin to feed the cording through the sewn portion of the handle. The cording will be slightly shorter than the sewn channel. **FIG.C**

8. Position the open edge of the handle on the right side of 1 exterior piece, 3″ down from the top edge and 5¼″ in from the side. Pin and sew ¼″ from the bottom of the handle. Repeat on the opposite end of the handle. If you are working on the side with the zipper pocket, take care to keep the zipper pocket fabric away from the stitching. **FIG.D**

9. Press the handle up over the stitch line and pin in place. Mark and sew a 1″ box on the end of the handle to secure it. **FIG.E**

10. Repeat Steps 3–9 with the remaining handle and second exterior piece.

11. Match the exterior bag pieces, right sides together. Clip or pin the bottom only and sew.

B. Fold handle in half over seam and pin.

C. Feed cord through handle.

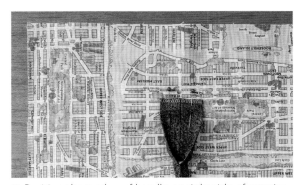

D. Position short edge of handle on right side of exterior.

E. Press handle up and mark stitch lines.

Trim the foam interfacing from the seam allowance and press open. **FIG.F**

Skip to Step 16 if you are not sewing the optional bag bottom.

12. Draw lines on the wrong side of the bag bottom ½″ in from the 10″ edges. Fold the long edges over to the lines and hold in place with clips. **FIG.G**

13. Increase your stitch length and sew close to the raw edges to secure the folded edge. A Teflon or rolling presser foot can help. You also may need to use a machine needle made for the material you are using.

14. Match the wrong side of the bag bottom to the right side of the bottom of the exterior, centered over the bottom seam. The short edges of the bag bottom will line up with the inset for the corners. Clip the short edges to the exterior. **FIG.H**

F. Match exterior bag pieces right sides together and clip bottom.

G. Draw line on wrong side of bag bottom and match long edge to it.

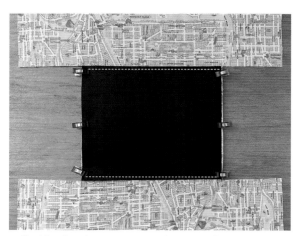

H. Position bag bottom on exterior, centering over bottom seam.

15. Sew along a long edge of the bag bottom, through the exterior. Repeat on the opposite edge.

16. Match the exterior pieces at the sides, right sides together. Pin and sew. Trim the foam interfacing from the seam allowances and press open.

17. Create the bottom corners of the purse by matching a side seam to the bottom bag seam. Pin and sew in a straight line. Repeat with the opposite corner. Turn right side out and set aside. **FIG.I**

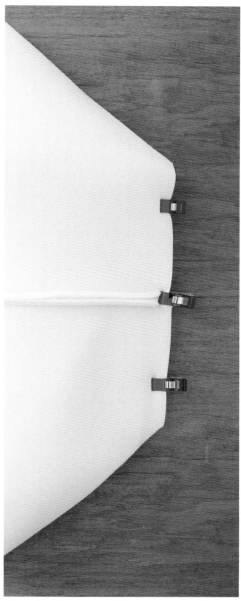

I. Match side seam and bottom seam, right sides together, to form bag corners.

18. Fold 1 tubular frame casing in half, right sides together, matching the long edges. Stitch the short edges closed with a ½˝ seam allowance. Trim the seam allowances to reduce bulk. Turn right side out and press. Baste the long open edge closed. **FIG.J**

19. Match the basted edge of the tubular frame casing, centered, to the top edge of the right side of the exterior. The purse frame will run between the casing and the bag, and the finished edge of the casing will be ½˝ in from the hinge of the purse frame to allow it to open and close smoothly. Baste. **FIG.K**

20. Repeat Steps 18 and 19 with the remaining tubular frame casing on the other side of the exterior.

21. Make 2 patch pockets (page 28) using the 10˝ × 10˝ pocket squares. Sew 1 pocket to each lining piece, positioning them 5˝ up from the bottom edge and 5½˝ in from the left edge.

22. Repeat Steps 11, 16, and 17 to assemble the lining, but leave an 8˝ gap in the bottom of the lining for turning the bag right side out.

23. Slip the purse exterior into the lining, right sides together, and match the top edges of the bags. Pin and sew. **FIG.L**

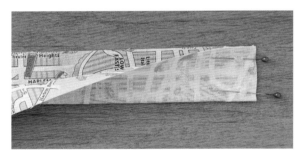

J. Fold and match tubular frame casing, right sides together.

K. Baste tubular frame casing to top edge of exterior.

L. Insert bag exterior and handles into lining, right sides together.

24. Turn the purse right side out through the gap in the lining. Press well, making sure the lining is fully tucked inside the bag.

25. Press the tubular frame casing down toward the lining. Pin and sew close to the bottom edge of the casing to secure. Repeat with the other tubular frame casing.

26. Slipstitch or machine stitch the gap in the lining closed.

27. Follow the package directions to insert the tubular frame into the casing.

boat/pool tote

Boat/Pool Tote pattern

FINISHED TOTE: 17½″ wide at bottom (20½″ wide at top) × 11¼″ high × 6″ deep

Materials

Yardage is based on 42″ width of fabric unless stated otherwise.

LAMINATED COTTON:
⅜ yard, 54″ wide, for exterior

QUILTING COTTON:
- 1 yard for lining
- ⅓ yard for pocket

INTERFACING:
- ⅜ yard foam interfacing, 58″ wide
- ¾ yard woven fusible interfacing, 20″ wide (or ⅓ yard, 44″ wide)

ELASTIC: ⅓ yard, ⅜″ wide

DOUBLE-FOLD BINDING:
1½ yards, ½″ wide

NYLON WEBBING:
2½ yards, 1″–1½″ wide

Cutting

See Pattern Tip (page 36).

EXTERIOR AND FOAM INTERFACING
- Cut 2 rectangles 27″ × 14½″. Angle a ruler from the top corner to 1½″ in at the bottom corner and cut the side at an angle. Repeat on the opposite side. Cut 1 square 3″ × 3″ from each bottom corner.

LINING
- Cut 1 rectangle 29″ × 14½″. Subcut into 3 pieces: 1 rectangle 15″ × 14½″ and 2 rectangles 6½″ × 14½″. (*This half will be trimmed to size after attaching an in-seam pocket.*)
- Cut 1 rectangle 27″ × 14½″. Angle a ruler from the top corner to 1½″ in at the bottom corner and cut the side at an angle. Repeat on the opposite side. Cut 1 square 3″ × 3″ from each bottom corner.

POCKET
- Cut 2 rectangles 10″ × 21″.

WOVEN FUSIBLE INTERFACING
- Cut 1 rectangle 10″ × 21″.

WEBBING
- Cut into 2 equal-length pieces.

Inside the / **hack**

Angling the sides of the Basic Tote Bag (page 36) makes a larger, more accessible opening. Water-resistant straps wrap around from the bottom for extra support. Laminated cotton fabric helps keep what's inside the bag from getting wet.

All seam allowances are ¼″ unless otherwise noted. Refer to Anatomy of the Tote Bag Pattern (page 8) and the Glossary (page 99) as needed. When using laminated cotton, use clips or pin only in the seam allowances. Finger-press. If necessary, iron from the wrong side, on low heat only, using a pressing cloth.

1. Fuse the woven fusible interfacing to the wrong side of 1 of the pocket pieces.

2. Match the interfaced and noninterfaced pocket pieces, right sides together, and sew the top edge. Press the seam allowance open. Press the pocket flat, wrong sides together.

3. Baste the bottom edge of the pocket and finish the seam allowance with a serger, mock overlock stitch, or zigzag stitch close to the raw edge.

4. Topstitch close to the top edge of the pocket and again ⅝″ below the top line of stitching.

5. Mark the center bottom of the pocket.

6. Sew 2 parallel rows of gathering stitches within the seam allowance of the pocket bottom.

7. Measure and mark a line 4″ up from the bottom edge on the right side of the 15″ × 14½″ lining rectangle. Mark the center of the lining. Center the bottom edge of the pocket, wrong (noninterfaced) side up on the mark. The top edge of the pocket will extend past the bottom edge of the lining piece. **FIG. A**

8. Pin the pocket center mark to the center mark on the lining. Pull the gathering stitches until the pocket fits the width of the lining rectangle. Pin. Sew ¼″ from the bottom edge of the pocket. **FIG. B**

A. Place pocket on lining piece, aligning with mark.

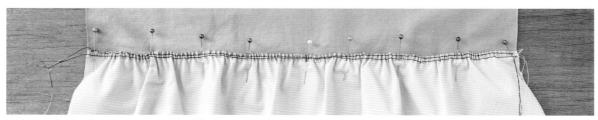

B. Gather pocket bottom to fit width of lining.

9. Press the pocket up, covering the finished edge.

10. Use a bodkin or safety pin to insert the elastic through the casing at the top edge of the pocket.

11. Baste the sides of the pocket and the elastic to the lining rectangle. **FIG.C**

12. Match a 6½″ × 14½″ lining rectangle to the pocket/lining section along the long edges, right sides together. Sew. Press the seam allowances away from the pocket. **FIG.D**

C. Baste sides of pocket to lining.

D. Assemble lining pieces, right sides together.

13. Repeat the previous step with the opposite side of the pocket/lining section and the remaining 6½″ × 14½″ lining rectangle.

14. Follow the cutting instructions to trim the sides and bottom corners of the assembled pocket/lining piece to match the other lining piece.

15. Baste a corresponding foam interfacing piece to the wrong side of each lining piece.

16. Match the lining pieces, right sides together, and pin or clip the sides and bottom. Sew. Press the seams open and trim the foam from the seam allowances if needed.

17. Match the side seam of the lining to the bottom seam to create the bag corners. Pin or clip and sew in a straight line. Repeat with the opposite corner.

18. Measure 4¾″ in from the inside edge of the corner at the bottom of a right-side-up exterior piece. Pin the handle to the exterior, aligning the raw edges. **FIGS. E & F**

19. Arc the handle up past the top of the exterior and align the remaining raw edge with the bottom of the bag, 4¾″ in from the inside edge of the opposite corner. Pin.

E. Place handle on exterior and pin.

F. Place handle on exterior and pin.

G. Baste exterior and lining around top edge of tote.

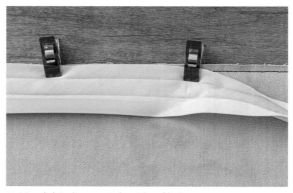

H. Match binding to right side of lining.

20. Stitch the handle to the exterior close to the edges, stopping 9″ up from bottom. Pivot to sew across the handle, pivot again, and continue sewing to the bottom.

21. Repeat Steps 18–20 with the remaining handle and exterior.

22. Repeat Steps 16 and 17 to assemble the exterior. Turn the exterior right side out.

23. Place the lining inside the exterior, wrong sides together. Match and clip or pin the top edges, aligning the side seams. Baste all the way around the top edge. **FIG. G**

24. Measure the top of the tote, add ½″ for the seam allowance, and cut the binding to fit.

25. Match the short edges of the binding and sew. Press open the seam allowance.

26. Unfold the binding. Match the right side of the binding against the right side of the lining. Clip and sew. **FIG. H**

27. Fold the binding over the top edge of the tote, folding the raw edge to the inside. Clip and sew close to the bottom folded edge of the binding.

messenger
bag with flap

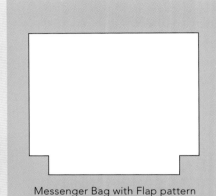

Messenger Bag with Flap pattern

FINISHED BAG: 13″ wide × 12¾″ high × 4″ deep

Materials

Yardage is based on 42″ width of fabric unless stated otherwise.

FABRIC:

- ☐ ¾ yard for exterior and zipper pocket
- ☐ ⅝ yard for lining and removable bottom insert
- ☐ ½ yard for flap, strap, and tabs
- ☐ ⅓ yard for patch pocket

FUSIBLE FLEECE: ¾ yard, 45″ wide

INTERFACING:

- ☐ 1¼ yards woven fusible interfacing, 20″ wide
- ☐ ⅛ yard foam interfacing, 58″ wide (or scrap at least 1½″ × 42″)

ZIPPER: 14″ long

HEAVYWEIGHT CRAFT STABILIZER: 3½″ × 12¾″ piece

O-RINGS: 2 at 1½″ diameter

TURN-LOCK PURSE CLASP: 1

ADJUSTABLE SLIDE BUCKLE: 1½″ wide

Inside the / **hack**

This bag has smaller corners than the Basic Tote Bag (page 36) to make this hack narrower, which works well for the added flap closure. A single adjustable strap connects to tabs with O-rings on the sides of the bag.

All seam allowances are ¼″ unless otherwise noted. Refer to Anatomy of the Tote Bag Pattern (page 8) and the Glossary (page 99) as needed.

Cutting

See Pattern Tip (page 36).

EXTERIOR

☐ Cut 2 rectangles 17½″ × 15″. Cut a 2″ × 2″ square from each bottom corner.

☐ **Zipper pocket:** Cut 2 rectangles 12″ × 9″.

LINING

☐ Cut 2 rectangles 17½″ × 15″. Cut a 2″ × 2″ square from each bottom corner.

☐ **Bottom insert:** Cut 2 rectangles 13¼″ × 4¼″.

PATCH POCKETS

☐ Cut 2 rectangles 12″ × 9″.

FLAP, STRAP, AND TABS

☐ **Flap and flap lining:** Cut 2 rectangles 12″ × 13½″

☐ **Strap:** Cut 2 rectangles 2″ × 42″.

☐ **Tabs:** Cut 1 rectangle 5″ × 11″.

FUSIBLE FLEECE

☐ **Exterior:** Cut 2 rectangles 17½″ × 15″. Cut 1 square 2″ × 2″ from each bottom corner.

☐ **Flap:** Cut 1 rectangle 12″ × 13½″

FUSIBLE WOVEN INTERFACING

☐ **Lining:** Cut 2 rectangles 17½″ × 15″. Cut 1 square 2″ × 2″ from each bottom corner.

☐ **Flap lining:** Cut 1 rectangle 12″ × 13½″

☐ **Patch pocket:** Cut 1 rectangle 12″ × 9″.

☐ **Tabs:** Cut 1 rectangle 2½″ × 11″.

FOAM INTERFACING

☐ **Strap:** Cut 1 rectangle 1½″ × 42″.

1. Follow the manufacturer's directions to fuse the fleece and woven fusible interfacing to the wrong sides of the corresponding pieces.

2. Use the 12″ × 9″ zipper pocket rectangles to make a zippered pocket (page 30) on 1 exterior piece with a ½″ × 9″ rectangular zipper window. Position the zipper window 3½″ down from the top edge and centered from side to side.

3. Match the exterior bag pieces, right sides together. Pin the bottom and sides and sew. Press open the seam allowances.

4. Make a bottom corner of the bag by matching the side seam to the bottom bag seam. Pin and sew in a straight line. Repeat with the opposite corner. Turn right side out and set the bag aside. **FIG. A**

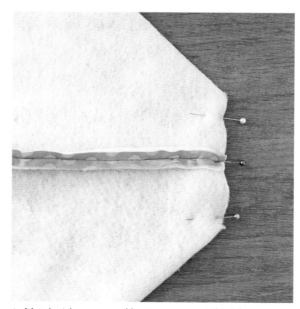

A. Match side seam and bottom seam, right sides together, to form bag corners.

5. Refer to Patch Pockets (page 28) to make a patch pocket with the 12″ × 9″ pocket rectangles. Sew the pocket to a lining piece, positioning it 5″ up from the bottom edge and 3″ from the left edge.

6. Repeat Steps 3 and 4 to assemble the lining, but leave a 5″ gap in the bottom of the lining for turning the bag right side out.

7. Match the flap and flap lining, right sides together. Use or a CD or DVD or a compass set to 4¾″ diameter to mark and trim the curved bottom corners of the flap 2″ from each side of the corner. **FIG.B**

8. Pin the sides and bottom of the flap and flap lining right sides together and sew. Clip the curve, turn right side out, and press.

9. Topstitch close to the edge around the sides and bottom of the flap. Baste the top edge closed.

10. Follow the manufacturer's directions to install the female portion of the turn-lock clasp on the flap 2″ up from the bottom edge, centered.

11. Baste the top edge of the flap to the top edge of the back side of the bag exterior, with the outer side of the flap toward the right side of the exterior. **FIG.C**

12. Fold the tab rectangle in half, wrong sides together, matching the long edges. Press.

13. Open the tab rectangle and press the raw long edges in to the center. Open and place the woven fusible interfacing in the center of the tab. Refold the tab and press to fuse. **FIG.D**

B. Curve bottom corners of flap.

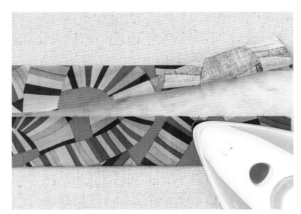

D. Place woven fusible interfacing in center of tab.

C. Match top edge of flap to top edge of exterior back.

14. Fold the tab on the center crease so the raw edges are hidden inside. Stitch close to the open long edge to secure. Repeat on the remaining long edge. If desired, sew another line of stitches ¼″ from each long edge.

15. Cut the tab in half to create 2 pieces 1¼″ × 5½″.

16. Insert a tab through an O-ring. Match the raw edges and baste. Sew close to the O-ring through both layers of the tab. Repeat this step with the second tab and O-ring.

17. Match the raw edge of the tab to the top edge of the exterior, centering it over the side

seam. Baste. Repeat with the second tab on the opposite side seam. **FIG.E**

18. Slip the bag exterior into the lining, right sides together, and match the top edges of the bags. The patch pocket should be on the same side of the bag as the flap. Pin all around, matching the side seams, and sew. **FIG.F**

19. Turn the bag right side out through the gap in the lining. Press well, making sure the lining is fully tucked inside the bag.

20. Topstitch around the top edge of the bag, making sure the flap and tabs are out of the way.

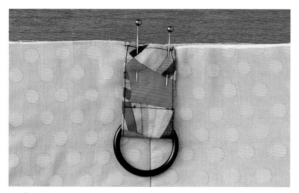

E. Center tab over side seam and baste.

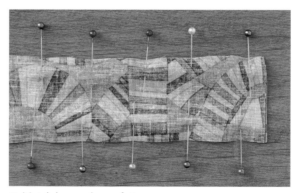

G. Match long edges of strap.

F. Insert bag exterior and straps into bag lining, right sides together.

21. Fold the flap over the front of the bag and mark the placement for the male end of the turn-lock clasp. Follow the manufacturer's directions for installing the clasp, taking care to move the bottom of the zipper pocket out of the way.

22. Slipstitch or machine stitch the gap in the lining closed.

23. Match the strap rectangles, right sides together, and pin the long edges. Sew. Turn right side out and press well. **FIG.G**

24. Use a bodkin or safety pin to feed the foam interfacing through the strap. Sew close to the long edges to secure. If desired, sew a second row of stitches ¼˝ from each long edge.

25. Press the short edges of the strap ¼˝ to one side of the strap. Attach to the adjustable strap buckle, following the package directions.

26. Refer to Removable Bottom Insert (page 34) to make and insert the bottom insert with the corresponding fabric and craft stabilizer pieces.

zippered
cross-body
bag

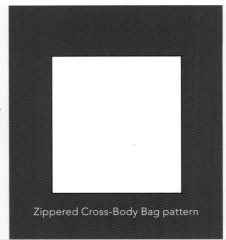

Zippered Cross-Body Bag pattern

FINISHED BAG: 10″ wide × 11″ high

Materials

Yardage is based on 42″ width of fabric unless stated otherwise.

QUILTING COTTON:
- ⅜ yard for exterior, ring tabs, and strap ends
- ⅜ yard for lining
- ⅛ yard for zipper tabs and pocket binding

COTTON WEBBING: 1½–2 yards, 1″ wide, for strap

INTERFACING: ⅞ yard woven fusible interfacing, 20″ wide (or ⅓ yard, 44″ wide)

FUSIBLE FLEECE: ⅓ yard, 45″ wide

ZIPPERS: 2 at 12″–14″ long

D-RINGS: 2 at 1¼″ wide

SWIVEL HOOKS WITH LOOPS: 2 at 1¼″ wide

ADJUSTABLE STRAP BUCKLE: 1¼″ wide

Inside the / **hack**

Removing the corners from the Basic Tote Bag (page 36) and adding a zipper closure to the top gives this bag a completely different look. A flush-zipper pocket on the front and a drop-in pocket on the back are finished with binding. Swivel hooks attach an adjustable strap to D-rings sewn into the top edge of the bag.

Cutting

See Pattern Tip (page 36).

EXTERIOR

☐ **Front top and front bottom:**
Cut 2 rectangles 10½″ × 6″.

☐ **Back:** Cut 1 rectangle 10½″ × 11½″.

☐ **Back pocket:** Cut 1 rectangle 10½″ × 7″.

☐ **Ring tabs:** Cut 1 rectangle 4″ × 8″.

☐ **Strap ends:** Cut 2 rectangles 1½″ × 2″.

LINING

☐ **Front and back lining:**
Cut 2 rectangles 10½″ × 11½″.

☐ **Back pocket lining:**
Cut 1 rectangle 10½″ × 7″.

☐ **Zipper pocket inner lining:**
Cut 1 rectangle 10½″ × 6″.

☐ **Zipper pocket outer lining:**
Cut 1 rectangle 10½″ × 6″.

☐ **Zipper tabs:** Cut 4 rectangles 1″ × 2″.

POCKET BINDING AND ZIPPER TABS

☐ **Pocket binding:** Cut 1 rectangle 10½″ × 2″

☐ **Zipper tabs:** Cut 4 rectangles 1″ × 2″.

FUSIBLE FLEECE

☐ **Front top and front bottom:**
Cut 2 rectangles 10½″ × 6″.

☐ **Back:** Cut 1 rectangle 10½″ × 11½″.

☐ **Back pocket:** Cut 1 rectangle 10½″ × 7″.

INTERFACING

☐ **Front and back lining:**
Cut 2 rectangles 10½″ × 11½″.

☐ **Back pocket lining:**
Cut 1 rectangle 10½″ × 7″.

☐ **Zipper pocket inner lining:**
Cut 1 rectangle 10½″ × 6″.

☐ **Zipper pocket outer lining:**
Cut 1 rectangle 10½″ × 6″.

☐ **Ring tabs:** Cut 1 rectangle 2″ × 8″.

Construction

All seam allowances are ¼″ unless otherwise noted. Refer to Anatomy of the Tote Bag Pattern (page 8) and the Glossary (page 99) as needed.

1. Follow the manufacturer's directions to fuse the fusible fleece to the wrong side of each corresponding exterior piece and interfacing to the wrong side of each corresponding lining piece.

2. Match the back pocket and back pocket lining, wrong sides together. Pin and baste all 4 sides within the seam allowance.

3. Fold the pocket binding rectangle in half, wrong sides together, matching the long edges. Press. Match the long raw edges to the center and press. Fold the pocket binding in half. **FIG. A**

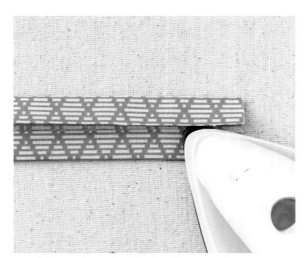

A. Fold raw edges of pocket binding toward center.

4. Sandwich the top edge of the back pocket inside the pocket binding. Pin. Sew close to the bottom folded edge of the pocket binding through all the layers from the front of the back pocket.

5. Place the back pocket on top of the back exterior, with the wrong side of the pocket against the right side of the back exterior. Match and pin the sides and bottom edges. Baste within the seam allowance. **FIG.B**

6. Fold the ring tab rectangle in half, wrong sides together, matching the long edges.

Press. Open up the fold, match the long raw edges to the center, and press.

7. Open the ring tab and place the corresponding woven fusible interfacing in the center. Fold the raw edges over the interfacing. Press to fuse the interfacing. **FIG.C**

8. Fold in half lengthwise so raw edges are inside and press again. Stitch close to the long open edge to secure. Repeat on the opposite edge. If desired, stitch a second row of stitches ¼˝ from each long edge.

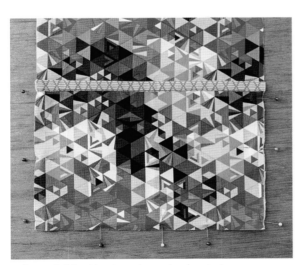

B. Baste finished back pocket to back exterior.

C. Fuse interfacing to ring tab.

9. Cut the ring tab in half to create 2 pieces 1″ × 4″.

10. Insert 1 ring tab through a D-ring. Match the short edges and pin. Sew close to the bottom of the D-ring through all the layers of the ring tab. Baste the short edges closed.

11. Repeat with the second ring tab and D-ring.

12. Align the short edge of the ring tab with the top edge of the back exterior, right sides together. The ring tab should be 1″ in from the side of the back. Baste. Repeat with the remaining ring tab on the opposite side of the top edge of the back. **FIG.D**

13. Remove the zipper from the package and press the tape flat with a medium-heat iron.

14. Open the zipper and use a hand-sewing needle and thread to stitch the zipper teeth together just below the top zipper stop.

15. Sandwich the top of the zipper between a contrast and a lining zipper tab, with the fabrics right sides together and the zipper's right side toward the contrast fabric. Align the right-hand ends of the zipper tabs with the hand stitching and pin in place. **FIG.E**

16. Sew ¼″ from the right-hand edge of the zipper tabs through all the layers. Trim the excess zipper even with the zipper tab seam allowance.

17. Press the zipper tabs over the seam allowance and topstitch close to the seam through all the layers. **FIG.F**

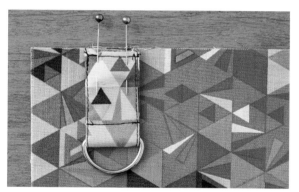

D. Baste ring tabs to top edge of back.

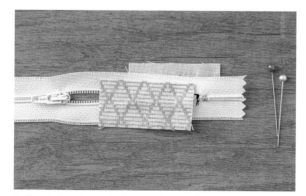

E. Sandwich zipper between zipper tabs.

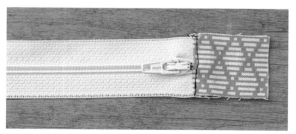

F. Topstitch close to seam through all layers.

18. Measure and mark 9¾″ from the finished inner end of the finished zipper tab. Repeat Steps 15–17, this time aligning the *left-hand* ends of the zipper tabs with the mark. The finished exposed zipper should measure 9½″. The excess tabs will be trimmed later.

19. Repeat Steps 15–18 with the second zipper and remaining zipper tabs.

20. Place a zipper with zipper tabs at the top edge of the zipper pocket outer lining, right side up, matching the wrong side of the zipper with the right side of the lining. **FIG.G**

21. Match the front bottom exterior to the zipper/lining piece, right sides together. Pin through all the layers across the top. Using a zipper foot, sew through all the layers close to

the zipper teeth, stopping two-thirds across to slide the zipper head out of the way. **FIG.H**

22. Press the fabric away from the zipper and topstitch along the edge of the exterior fabric from one edge to the other through all the layers.

23. Align the top edge of the zipper pocket inner lining with the top edge of the zipper on the front bottom/pocket piece from the previous step, right sides together. **FIG.I**

24. Align the bottom edge of the front top exterior with the top edge of the zipper on the front bottom/pocket, right sides together. Pin through all the layers. Sew through all the layers close to the zipper teeth, stopping two-thirds across to slide the zipper head out of the way. **FIG.J**

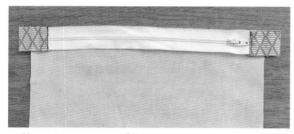

G. Place zipper on top of lining.

H. Match front bottom to zipper, right sides together.

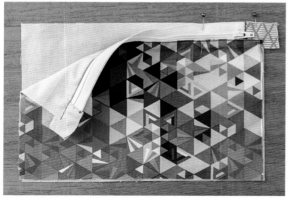

I. Align zipper pocket inner lining with remaining edge of zipper on front bottom/pocket.

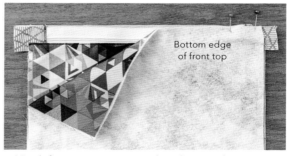

Bottom edge of front top

J. Match front top to zipper, right sides together.

25. Press the front top up away from the zipper. Topstitch along the edge of the exterior fabric from one side to the other through all the layers. Trim the zipper tabs and the excess of the bottom and lining. **FIG.K**

26. Fold the front bottom out of the way. Match the bottom edges of the zipper pocket inner and outer lining pieces. Pin and sew with a ½˝ seam allowance. **FIG.L**

27. Repeat Steps 20–22 to sew the top edge of the front top and front lining to the remaining zipper with zipper tabs. Sew the back and back lining pieces to the other side of the same zipper.

28. Open the upper zipper. Match the bag exterior pieces, right sides together, and bag lining pieces, right sides together.

29. Sew around all 4 edges, leaving a 4˝ gap in the bottom of the lining for turning right side out. Pinch the extra bulk from the zipper tabs up toward the exterior. **FIG.M**

30. Clip the bottom corners. Turn the bag right side out through the lining.

31. Push the lining into the bag and press. Slipstitch or machine stitch the opening in the lining closed.

K. Trim zipper tabs and excess of bottom and lining.

L. Match bottom edge of front bottom pocket with front bottom lining.

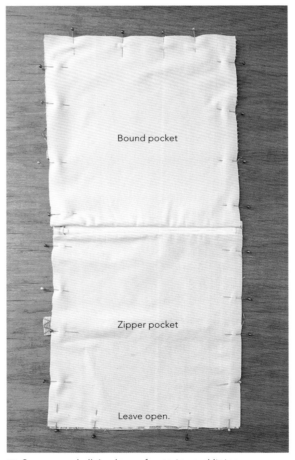

Bound pocket

Zipper pocket

Leave open.

M. Sew around all 4 edges of exterior and lining.

32. Press the strap ends in half, wrong sides together, matching the long edges. Open and press the raw edges toward the center crease. **FIG.N**

33. Fold the strap ends in half, right sides together, so the long raw edges are on the outside. Stitch across the short ends with a ¼″ seam allowance. Trim the seam allowance close to the stitching, turn right side out, and press. **FIG.O**

34. Check the length of the webbing by running it over a shoulder and across your body to see if you'd like to cut the strap shorter. Don't forget that you'll be adding an adjustable buckle. Slip the strap ends over the ends of the Strap and pin in place. Sew close to the opening of the strap ends, through all the layers. **FIG.P**

35. Wrap an end of the strap through the center bar of the adjustable strap buckle, fold it over 2″, and stitch together through the strap end. Feed the free end of the strap through the swivel hook loop and then back through the buckle as shown. **FIG.Q**

36. Insert the opposite end of the strap through the remaining swivel hook loop. Fold the strap over on itself and sew through the short edge to secure; then sew another line ¼″ from the edge.

37. Fasten the strap to the D-rings on the bag with the swivel hooks.

N. Press raw edges of strap ends toward center crease.

O. Sew across short ends of strap ends.

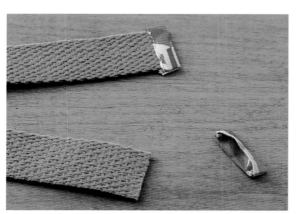

P. Sew strap ends to bottom of strap.

Q. Feed strap through swivel hook loop and adjustable strap buckle.

zip-top purse

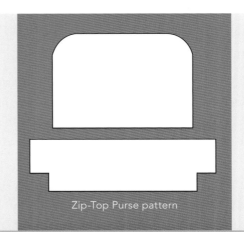

Zip-Top Purse pattern

FINISHED PURSE: 13¼″ wide × 11″ high × 4″ deep

Materials

Yardage is based on 42″ width of fabric unless stated otherwise.

FABRIC:

- ☐ ½ yard for exterior and gusset
- ☐ ⅝ yard for lining
- ☐ ¼ yard for patch pockets

KRAFT•TEX (BY C&T PUBLISHING), VINYL, LEATHER, OR HEAVYWEIGHT FABRIC: ¼ yard for contrast base

INTERFACING:

- ☐ ½ yard foam interfacing, 58″ wide
- ☐ 1¼ yards woven fusible interfacing, 20″ wide

ZIPPER: 30″ long

HANDLES: 23″ long

WOOD OR CHIPBOARD: 3⅞″× 13″ piece for bag bottom

PURSE FEET: 4

Cutting

See Pattern Tip (page 36).

NOTE: Some manufacturers sell yardage that matches their ready-made purse handles. You can also make your own handles following the instructions in the Tubular Frame Purse (page 60).

EXTERIOR

- ☐ **Upper:**
  Cut 2 rectangles 9″ × 13¾″.
- ☐ **Gusset:**
  Cut 2 rectangles 2½″ × 32″.

LINING

- ☐ **Upper lining:**
  Cut 2 rectangles 9″ × 13¾″.
- ☐ **Gusset lining:**
  Cut 2 rectangles 2½″ × 32″.
- ☐ **Base lining:**
  Cut 2 rectangles 5″ × 17¾″.
  Cut 1 square 2″ × 2″ from each bottom corner.

PATCH POCKETS

- ☐ Cut 4 rectangles 8″ × 10″.

Inside the / hack

The addition of a zippered gusset between the bag body panels dramatically changes the look of the base pattern. A contrasting bottom panel, purse feet, and a lining add to the structured shape.

All seam allowances are ¼″ unless otherwise noted. Refer to Anatomy of the Tote Bag Pattern (page 8) and the Glossary (page 99) as needed.

CONTRAST

☐ **Base:**

Cut 2 rectangles 5″ × 17¾″. Cut 1 square 2″ × 2″ from each bottom corner.

FOAM INTERFACING

☐ **Upper:**

Cut 2 rectangles 9″ × 13¾″.

☐ **Gusset:**

Cut 2 rectangles 2½″ × 32″.

WOVEN FUSIBLE INTERFACING

☐ **Upper lining:**

Cut 2 rectangles 9″ × 13¾″.

☐ **Gusset lining:**

Cut 2 rectangles 2½″ × 32″.

☐ **Base lining:**

Cut 2 rectangles 5″ × 17¾″. Cut 1 square 2″ × 2″ from each bottom corner.

☐ **Patch pocket:**

Cut 2 rectangles 8″ × 10″.

1. Baste the foam interfacing to the wrong sides of the corresponding exterior upper and gusset panels. Follow manufacturer's directions to fuse the woven fusible interfacing to the lining, gusset lining, contrast lining, and 2 of the patch pockets.

2. Use a compass to draw a 4¾″ circle or trace a CD or DVD to mark and trim the top corners of the exterior upper pieces 2″ from each side of the corner. Repeat this step on the top corners of the lining upper pieces. **FIG. A**

3. Remove the zipper from the package and press the tape flat with a medium-heat iron.

4. Center the zipper on a gusset lining piece, both right sides up, matching the top edges.

5. Center a gusset piece, right side up, on top of the zipper tape, aligning the top edges to sandwich the zipper between the gusset and gusset lining. Pin or clip through all the layers. **FIG. B**

A. Curve top corners of exterior.

B. Sandwich zipper between gusset and gusset lining.

6. Using a zipper foot, sew close to the zipper teeth to attach the gusset to the zipper tape.

7. Press the fabric away from the zipper and topstitch along the edge of the fabric from one side to the other through all the layers. You may need to trim the foam interfacing from the seam allowance.

8. Repeat Steps 4–7 with the remaining gusset and gusset lining pieces and the other side of the zipper. The completed piece should measure 4½″ across. Trim if needed, keeping the zipper centered.

9. Match each interfaced pocket rectangle with a noninterfaced pocket rectangle to make 2 patch pockets (page 28). Sew 1 pocket to each upper lining piece, positioning them 1″

up from the bottom edge and 1¾″ from the left edge.

10. Follow the manufacturer's instructions to sew the ready-made handles to both exterior upper pieces by hand or machine, positioning them 1″ down and 2¼″ in from the sides. **FIG. C**

11. Starting in the center of each piece, match the raw edge of 1 gusset piece to 1 exterior piece, right sides together. Clip and baste.

12. Match 1 lining piece to the basted edge from Step 11, right sides together. Pin and sew. Trim the foam interfacing from the seam allowances. **FIG. D**

13. Repeat Steps 11 and 12 with the remaining raw edge of the gusset piece and second exterior and lining pieces. **FIG. E**

C. Position ready-made handles on exterior.

D. Sandwich gusset between exterior and lining.

E. Repeat Steps 11 and 12 with remaining exterior and lining pieces.

14. Match the short sides of the contrast base, right sides together. Pin and sew the sides but *not* the bottom. Press (or, if using vinyl, finger-press) the seam allowances open. **FIG.F**

15. Match the top of the contrast base to the bottom of the gusseted exterior, right sides together, aligning the contrast base side seam with the zipper. Clip or pin and sew all around. Trim any excess zipper tape, as well as the foam interfacing from the seam allowance. Press the seam allowance toward the exterior. **FIGS.G & H**

16. Open the zipper and turn the bag wrong side out.

17. Match the bottom of the contrast base, right sides together. Clip or pin and sew. Press open the seam allowance.

18. Create the bottom corners of the contrast base by matching a side seam to the bottom base seam. Clip or pin and sew in a straight line. Repeat with the opposite corner. Turn right side out. **FIG.I**

19. Drill holes for the purse feet in the hard bag bottom before placing it in the bag exterior.

20. Follow the manufacturer's directions for installing the purse feet.

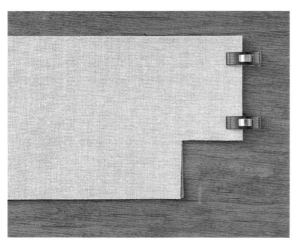

F. Sew sides but *not* bottom of contrast base.

G. Clip top of contrast base to bottom of gusseted exterior.

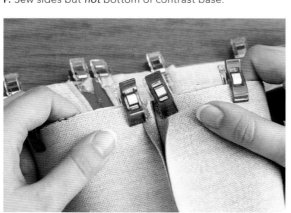

H. Use clips to hold open seam allowance.

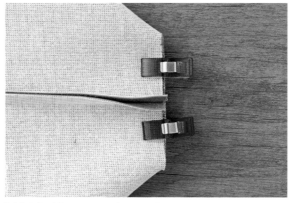

I. Match side seams to bottom bag seam to create corners.

21. Match the base lining pieces, right sides together. Pin and sew the side and bottom seams.

22. Create the bottom corners of the base lining by matching a side seam to the bottom seam. Pin and sew.

23. Press the top edge of the lining contrast ¼″ to the wrong side.

24. Insert the base lining into the bag, with the wrong side against the bottom of the contrast base. Use a hand-sewing needle to slipstitch the base lining to the upper lining.

laundry duffle bag

Laundry Duffle Bag pattern

FINISHED BAG: 14″ wide × 21¾″ high × 15″ deep

Materials

Yardage is based on 42″ width of fabric unless stated otherwise.

HEAVYWEIGHT FABRIC (COTTON CANVAS, COTTON DUCK, OR TWILL): 1¾ yards if usable width of fabric is less than 60″ (or 1¼ yards if greater than 60″)

INTERFACING: 1¾″ × 14½″ rectangle of heavyweight double-sided fusible interfacing (such as fast2fuse HEAVY Interfacing, by C&T Publishing)

CORDING: 1¾ yards

CORD-STOP FASTENER

Cutting

See Pattern Tip (page 36).

CANVAS

☐ Cut 2 squares 30″ × 30″.
Cut 1 square 7½″ × 7½″ from each bottom corner.

☐ **Drawstring casing:**
Cut 2 rectangles 2″ × 30″.

☐ **Handle:**
Cut 1 rectangle 8″ × 15½″.

Inside the / **hack**

Scaling up the Basic Tote Bag (page 36) yields the generous sizing of this Laundry Duffle Bag. Instead of shoulder straps, a single heavy-duty handle on the side of the bag makes it easy to carry. A drawstring casing enables the top of the bag to be cinched closed. Using a more utilitarian fabric allows you to skip the lining and finish the seams with a French seam instead.

Construction

All seam allowances are ¼″ unless otherwise noted. French seams (page 100) eliminate the need for a lining. Refer to Anatomy of the Tote Bag Pattern (page 8) and the Glossary (page 99) as needed.

1. Press the handle in half, wrong sides together, matching the long edges. Open up the handle and press both raw edges in to the center crease.

2. Open the handle and place the double-sided fusible interfacing between the center fold and 1 outer fold, leaving ½″ of extra fabric on each short end of the interfacing. Refold the handles and press to fuse the interfacing. **FIG.A**

3. Fold and press both noninterfaced ends of the handle to the wrong side, and then fold and press again so all raw edges are inside the handle.

4. Topstitch along both long edges. Sew a second line of topstitching ¼″ inside the first if desired. Set the handle aside.

5. Match the bag pieces, *wrong* sides together. Pin 1 side and sew. Trim the seam allowance to ⅛″.

6. Turn the bag right sides together and press the seam flat.

7. Sew the side seam a second time, capturing the trimmed seam allowances inside the stitching, to create a French seam (page 100). Press the seam allowance to one side.

8. With the finished seam right side up, measure 5″ down from the top edge of the bag and mark with chalk or removable fabric pen.

9. Measure 5″ up from the bottom edge of the side seam and make a second mark. **FIG.B**

A. Slip interfacing between center and outer fold.

B. Make placement marks for attaching handle.

10. Align the folded edges of the handle with the marks made in Steps 8 and 9, centering the handle over the seam. Pin in place.

11. Sew the handle to the bag with a 1½˝ box stitch as shown, connecting the corners by sewing an X. **FIG.C**

12. Repeat Steps 5–7 to sew the remaining side and bottom seams. Press both side seam allowances to the same side and the bottom seam allowance opposite. Turn the bag right side out.

13. Create the bottom corners of the Laundry Duffle Bag by matching the side seams to the bottom bag seam, *wrong* sides together. Pin and sew. Repeat with the opposite corner. Trim the seam allowances to ⅛˝. **FIG.D**

14. Turn the bag right sides together and press the seams flat.

15. Sew the bottom corners to create a French seam. Leave the bag wrong side out.

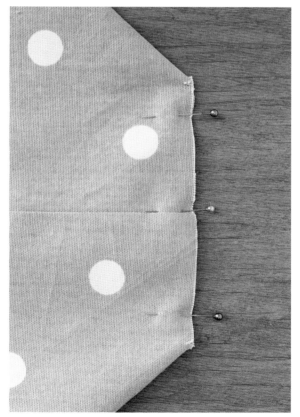

D. Match side seam and bottom seam, *wrong* sides together, to form bag corners.

C. Sew handle to bag.

16. Match the drawstring casing rectangles, right sides together. Pin and sew 1 short end with a ½˝ seam allowance.

17. Sew the opposite short end with a ½˝ seam allowance, stopping ½˝ from the top and bottom seams, leaving a 1˝ gap for the drawstring opening. Make sure to backstitch at the beginning and end of each line of stitches. It may help to mark the stitching line first. **FIG.E**

18. Press open the seam allowances. Press the raw edges of the seam allowance to the wrong side.

19. From the right side of the drawstring casing, topstitch along the seam allowances on both sides of the casing opening, making sure to catch both layers of the seam allowance. **FIG.F**

20. Press 1 raw edge of the drawstring casing ¼˝ to the wrong side.

21. Match the unpressed edge of the right side of the drawstring casing to the top edge of the wrong side of the duffle bag, aligning the side seams. Pin and sew all around. **FIG.G**

22. Press the drawstring casing over the seam allowance and flat against the exterior at the top of the duffle bag. Pin and sew close to the folded bottom edge of the drawstring casing.

23. Topstitch around the top edge of the drawstring casing.

24. Use a bodkin or safety pin to feed the cording through the drawstring casing. Push the cording ends through the cord-stop fastener. Knot the ends together.

E. Leave 1˝ gap between stitches on end of drawstring casing.

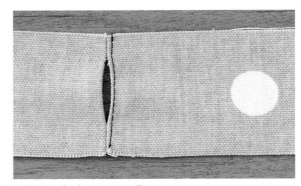

F. Topstitch along seam allowance.

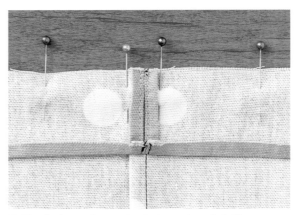

G. Match drawstring casing to top edge of duffle.

glossary

Here's a basic glossary of terms and techniques used in this book. With each technique definition, a brief "tutorial" provides how-to specifics. Many of the projects refer to techniques explained in this section, so you may find it helpful to bookmark ones that are unfamiliar, so you can locate them easily while sewing.

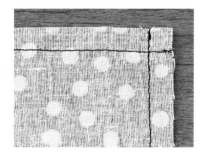

Backstitch

This machine stitch locks in the starting and ending stitches of a seam. At the beginning and end of each seam, sew forward 3–4 stitches. Use the reverse button or lever on your sewing machine and sew back along that line 3–4 stitches. Release the button and continue sewing. End each seam by backstitching 3–4 stitches.

Basting

Basting stitches are used to hold two or more pieces of fabric in place before you sew a seam. Basting allows you to test fit the placement before you do the final stitching. Set your sewing machine to the longest stitch length and sew as close to the edge as possible.

Buttonhole

A buttonhole is two parallel lines of tight zigzag stitches with end stitching (bar tacks) of wider zigzag stitching. Check your sewing machine manual for the available buttonhole stitches and the steps needed for your specific machine.

Notching

Curves

When you sew a curved seam, such as the flap of the Messenger Bag (page 74), get in the habit of keeping your eye on the presser foot and *not* on the sewing needle. Just take it slow and steady, guiding the fabric from in front of the presser foot without pushing it forward. It's okay to raise the presser foot and adjust the fabric on tight curves, but make sure the needle is in the down position (through the fabric), so it doesn't shift.

After stitching, curves are typically notched or clipped so the seam will lie properly after turning a piece right side out.

When you clip concave (inner) curves, carefully use the tip of your scissors to snip the fabric of the seam allowance perpendicular to your stitches. Take care not to snip through the stitches. Space the cuts about ⅓˝ apart through the curve.

On convex (outer) curves, cut triangular notches out of the seam allowance.

Flat lining

Layer one fabric with another fabric, wrong sides together. Baste around the raw edges, and then treat as one piece.

French seam

This seam treatment consists of two sets of stitching. The first seam is sewn with the fabric *wrong sides together*, using a ¼˝ seam allowance; and then trim the seam allowance to ⅛˝. The second seam is sewn with *right sides together*, again using a ¼˝ seam allowance. This creates a finished seam allowance with no visible raw edges that is pressed to the side. It's most often used with projects that are not lined, including the Laundry Duffle Bag (page 94) in this book.

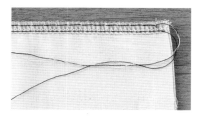

Gathering

To gather fabric, increase the machine's stitch length and sew two parallel rows of stitches within the seam allowance. Do not backstitch at either end. Pull the bobbin threads to gather the fabric to fit. Pin and sew to secure.

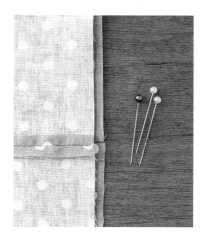

Matching seams

When sewing together pieces across seams, match the seams first and pin in place; then insert pins in between the seams. In a perfect world, the side and bottom seams will continue without interruption around the bag—but don't sweat it if they don't.

Pattern and fabric layout

Before cutting, match the selvage edges of your fabric and make sure there are no creases or wrinkles. Lay it on a flat surface in preparation for cutting.

NOTE: Always be sure to check the nap and/or the direction of the fabric print before cutting your pieces. One of my students ended up with a bag covered in upside-down cupcakes because she didn't double-check the orientation of her fabric before cutting the bag's corners!

If you make a pattern with tracing paper or another medium, use pattern weights or a few pins to hold the pattern to the fabric while you cut it with scissors or a rotary cutter. The fabric and pattern should stay as flat as possible while you cut. Don't lift up the fabric to cut around it. I try to cut near the corner of a table so I can move around the fabric and have access to as many sides as possible.

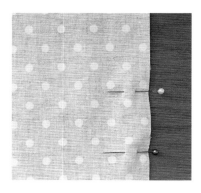

Pinning

Insert pins perpendicular to the seam, so that as you stitch you can easily remove them before they slide under the presser foot. Use fewer rather than more pins. They're just there to keep the pieces lined up as you maneuver them on your sewing machine. Using too many pins can actually create puckered fabric in your seams.

Pressing

Always start a project by ironing your fabric so it is nice and smooth before you start cutting the pattern.

Each project provides guidance for the direction to press the seam allowances. If you must press open the seam allowances, use your fingers to separate the seam allowance and iron down the middle, along the seam. I always turn the piece right side out and do a quick press on the right side, down the seam, to make sure I have not pressed in any puckers.

Rotary cutting

The fastest, most efficient way to cut basic shapes, such as squares and rectangles, is with a rotary cutter and acrylic ruler on a cutting mat. Hold down the ruler with the fingertips of your noncutting hand to help keep it from slipping. Always use great care—rotary cutters are razor sharp!

Seam allowance

The distance from the needle to the raw edge of the fabric is the seam allowance. Most projects in this book use a ¼˝ seam allowance.

Straight stitch

This is the most common stitch in your sewing arsenal, the one you'll use to construct almost everything you ever make (see the photo above). Keep your stitch to a short to medium length (I use 2.2) and sew with the edge of the fabric running along the mark on your sewing machine for the appropriate seam allowance (the projects in this book most often use a ¼˝ seam allowance).

Topstitching

Topstitching is both functional and decorative. It helps maintain the shape of your project and/or keeps seams flat on the inside. You can use a longer straight stitch (I set mine to 3.0) or a decorative stitch (zigzag or fancier). Stitches will be close to the seam or edge of a project.

Tip
When topstitching, I switch out my regular presser foot for a clear appliqué foot. It makes it easier to see the seams.

Resources

Most of the fabric used in this book can be found at independent quilt shops around the world.

LEATHER

Hide House
hidehouse.com

Tandy Leather Factory
tandyleather.com

VINYL

Once Upon a Yard
onceuponayard.com

Sy Fabrics
syfabrics.com

PURSE FRAMES

3D Hardwares
etsy.com/shop/3DANsupplies

Ghee's
ghees.com

PURSE HANDLES

Hobby & Land
hobbynland.com

About the Author

After an award-winning print journalism career spanning nearly two decades, Mary Abreu left the newsroom to pursue her passion for sewing. She has authored two previous books with Stash Books: first *Little Girls, Big Style* and then *Modern Style for Girls*. Mary also works as a seamstress with a boutique movie production company and has wardrobe department credits on two short films, including *The Candy Shop*, starring Doug Jones. She is an accomplished sewing instructor who teaches a wide range of classes. Mary enjoys attending pop culture conventions, where she is a regular presenter on the topics of pattern drafting and hacking, costuming for children, and historically influenced costuming. She lives with her family near Atlanta, Georgia. You can follow Mary on her blog, *Confessions of a Craft Addict*, at confessionsofacraftaddict.com.

Also by Mary Abreu:

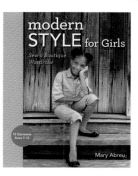

Want even more creative content?

Make it, snap it, share it
using
#ctpublishing